"His splendour covers the heavens
And the earth is full of his praise."
— Habakkuk 3:3

Portrait of a Forest

Richard Kraus

Constable London

First published in Great Britain
in 1986 by
Constable and Company Limited
10 Orange Street
London WC2 H7EG

Hardback ISBN 0 09 467490 6

Paperback ISBN 0 09 4662207

Copyright Richard Kraus

Printed in England by
Hazell Watson & Viney Ltd.

Colour Reproductions by
Aero Offset Reproductions Ltd.

Portrait of a Forest is a photographic study of the New Forest in southern England. The book follows the acclaimed publication of *An English Forest* with seventy-five new pictures.

The photographs journey through the cycle of one year and are all taken at dawn. The collection of pictures speak for themselves without the need for text.

"For the earth will be filled
With the glory of the Lord."
— Habakkuk 2:14